Directed Reading *6th grade*

Lesson: Self-Esteem and You

1. Feeling good about yourself even when you may not be the best player at a particular sport or other activity is a sign of a healthy

_______________________.

HOW YOU FEEL ABOUT YOURSELF

2. What is self-esteem?

____

____

______ **3.** A person with healthy self-esteem
  a. generally feels good about himself or herself.
  b. experiences some low levels of self-esteem.
  c. is more likely to be successful.
  d. All of the above

HIGH SELF-ESTEEM

4. What are some characteristics of a person with high self-esteem?

____

____

5. People with _______________________ self-esteem usually do not depend on the opinions of others to determine how they feel about themselves.

6. Knowing your weaknesses, and accepting them, is a characteristic of

someone with _______________________ self-esteem.

______ **7.** People with high self-esteem
  a. feel poorly about themselves.
  b. do not have weaknesses.
  c. are uncomfortable with their personalities.
  d. None of the above

Directed Reading *continued*

LOW SELF-ESTEEM

8. Someone who has _____________________ would be unhappy with his or her physical appearance.

_______ **9.** People with low self-esteem
   a. do not share certain traits.
   b. are not affected deeply by what others say.
   c. typically practice some unhealthy behaviors.
   d. feel good about themselves.

10. As you grow as a person, your _____________________ changes.

HOW PEOPLE AFFECT YOUR SELF-ESTEEM

11. As your self-esteem develops it is influenced by many factors. List three factors that would impact your self-esteem.

____

____

____

12. The amount of _____________________ you get from your family can affect your self-esteem.

13. Encouragement helps build a _____________________ level of self-esteem.

14. Peers can negatively impact your self-esteem by _____________________ or

_____________________ you at school.

_______ **15.** The person who influences your self-esteem the most is
   a. your family.
   b. yourself.
   c. your friends.
   d. your teachers.

THE MEDIA AND YOUR SELF-ESTEEM

16. Describe how the media can affect your self-esteem.

____

____

Directed Reading *continued*   *16th grade*

_______ **17.** Which of the following would be included in the media?
   a. television
   b. music videos
   c. movies
   d. All of the above

18. The way you see and imagine your body is called _____________________.

Lesson: Your Self-Concept

19. The way you see yourself as a person is called your _____________________.

WHAT IS SELF-CONCEPT

20. Self-concept is a part of self-esteem. Explain how self-concept is different from self-esteem.

____

____

21. If you see yourself as a writer for the local newspaper, this would be an

example of your _____________________.

22. If you feel good about being a writer for the newspaper this would be an

example of _____________________.

23. Your self-concept can affect your self-esteem. A _____________________

self-concept will help you will keep a healthy level of self-esteem.

HOW SELF-CONCEPT DEVELOPS

_______**24.** Self-concept develops from which different areas of your personality?
   a. academic self-concept
   b. physical self-concept
   c. social self-concept
   d. All of the above

25. How you see yourself in relationships, as a friend, for example, is your

_____________________ self-concept.

Match each area of your personality with the appropriate choice: write *A* for *academic self-concept*, *P* for *physical self-concept,* and *S* for *social self-concept.*

_______**26.** How you see yourself as a brother or sister

_______**27.** How you see yourself as a student

_______**28.** How you see yourself as a athlete

_______**29.** How you see yourself as a daughter or son

_______**30.** How you see yourself as a classmate

31. As you grow emotionally, your overall _______________________ will change.

32. A positive self-concept will help you have a healthy

_______________________.

Lesson: Building Self-Esteem

33. When we do something that makes us feel bad about ourselves, we need to know how to make ourselves feel better and build healthier

_______________________.

THREE KEYS TO HEALTHY SELF-ESTEEM

34. What are three ways to build character and healthy self-esteem?

____

____

____

_______**35.** What is a positive way to build healthy self-esteem?
  a. respecting yourself
  b. being hard on yourself
  c. being aggressive
  d. being feared by others

36. Your ability to take responsibility for your actions is your _______________.

37. Knowing what is _______________ for you and what is

_______________ for you is called respecting yourself.

38. When you act on your thoughts and values in an honest and respectful way

you are being _______________.

| Directed Reading *continued*   6th grade.

SEVEN WAYS TO HEALTHY SELF-ESTEEM

39. Asking questions to get to ___________________ can make developing
integrity and respecting yourself easier.

40. When you don't want to change your personality too much, you've made the

step to ___________________.

**Match one of the following seven ways to build healthy self-esteem below with
statements 41–44**

_______**41.** Deciding what kind of things
you like

_______**42.** Volunteering at a local charity

_______**43.** Spending time at a hobby you
enjoy

_______**44.** Following a plan to its end

a. getting to know yourself

b. accepting yourself

c. being good at something

d. setting a goal

e. being positive

f. turning problems into challenges

g. doing something for others

Concept Mapping

Lesson: Self-Esteem and You

Use the following terms to complete the concept map below: *school, healthy, respect yourself, relationships, feel self-confident about yourself, self-esteem, facing new situations,* **and** *value yourself.*

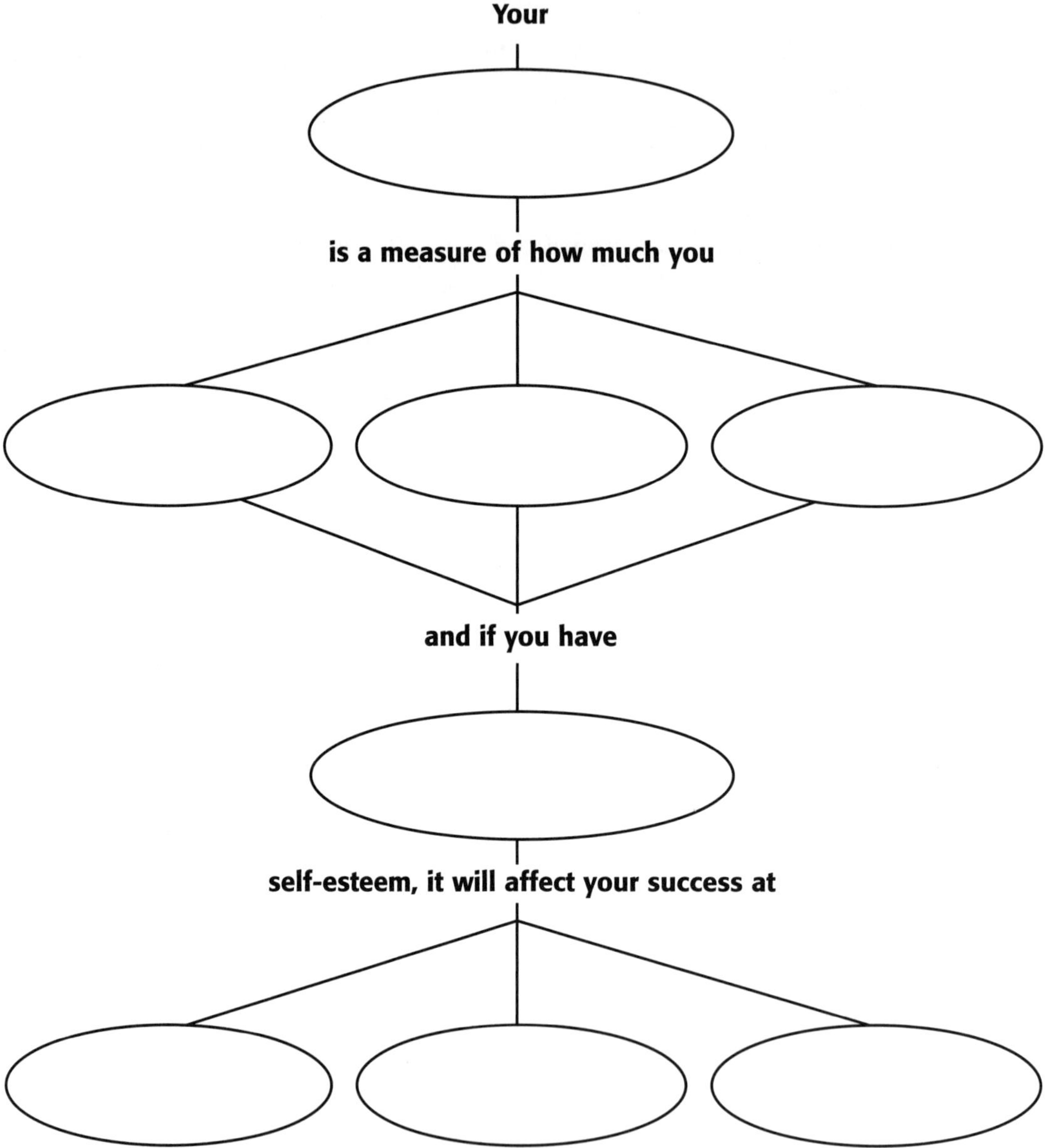

Concept Mapping

Lesson: Your Self-Concept

Use the following terms to create a concept map in the space below: *self-esteem, academic, social, self-concept, friend, athlete, student, physical,* **and** *relationships.*

<u>Skills Worksheet</u>

Concept Review

Lesson: Self-Esteem and You

In the blanks provided, write *HSE* next to the scenario which encourages healthy self-esteem or *LSE* next to the scenario which fosters low self-esteem.

_______ **1.** You are proud of the perfect grades you get on tests. Today your teacher passed back the Chapter Test and you got a B+. You realize you could have done better, but are not mad at yourself.

_______ **2.** Even though most of your friends order burgers and pizza, you enjoy ordering salad because it's good for you and it makes you feel good to be an individual.

_______ **3.** You saw your friend whisper something to another classmate. You're sure they're making plans and you're not going to be invited to come along.

_______ **4.** At your ball game, you look over at the sidelines and don't see your parents. Usually they come and cheer, but they had an important meeting to attend and knew you'd be okay if they missed one game.

_______ **5.** After a haircut, someone says to you, "Did you have your ears lowered?" but you feel good about how you look, so you just smile.

_______ **6.** Your friends tell you that you look like a famous musician. You're not so sure you really do, but you appreciate the comparison and your friends' interest in you.

_______ **7.** You've stopped brushing your teeth in the morning because you can't stand looking in the mirror at your mouth full of braces and rubber bands.

_______ **8.** A group of guys are standing around smoking cigarettes, one of the group offers you one, you decline, one of them calls you a wimp. You laugh and respond, "Whatever."

_______ **9.** You are walking to class with your buddies, you trip in the hall, your buddies laugh, you laugh with them.

_______ **10.** You practiced for months to get on the team. Although you were not selected, you feel good about your effort and will try again next time.

11. Explain how the media can impact your level of self-esteem.

____

____

| Concept Review *continued*

---

12. Media, by usually showing only very successful and attractive people, can

hurt your ____________________________.

Lesson: Your Self-Concept

13. ____________________________ is how you feel about yourself.

14. ____________________________ is how you see and imagine yourself.

15. How you see yourself as a student is called your ____________________________.

16. How you see your physical abilities is called your ____________________________.

17. How you see yourself in relationships is called your ____________________________.

18. A ____________________________ self-concept may lead to an unhealthy level of

self-esteem.

**Match the area of self concept with the appropriate name. Use the letters *AS*
(academic), *PS* (physical), and *SS* (social) to identify the specific area of self-concept.**

____________________________ **19.** son/daughter

____________________________ **20.** student

____________________________ **21.** cheerleader

____________________________ **22.** brother

____________________________ **23.** swimmer

Lesson: Building Self-Esteem

24. List three key ways to build healthy self-esteem.

____

____

____

25. Taking responsibility for your actions is called ____________________________.

26. Acting on your thoughts and values with respect and honesty is called being

____________________________.

27. Knowing what is right and wrong is a way to ____________________________

yourself.

Concept Review *continued*

28. By knowing yourself, you can build healthy self-esteem. Knowing yourself

means understanding what your _____________________ and your

_____________________ are.

29. You can help people who need help by _____________________ your time,
effort, and energy.

30. Identify five ways to build healthy self-esteem.

____

____

____

____

____

Fill in the blanks with the appropriate letters to complete the words in 31–33

31. A way to healthy self-esteem that means being comfortable with your

appearance is __ C __ __ __ __ __ __ G yourself.

32. A way to healthy self-esteem that means following a plan for a certain

achievement called is __ __ T __ __ __ __ a goal.

33. A way to healthy self-esteem that means being your own personal cheerleader

is __ __ __ N G   __ O __ __ T __ __ __.

Refusal Skills

Lesson: Your Self-Concept

Describe how you would use the following refusal skills to respond to the following scenario. Remember to be clear and choose your words carefully. Be sure to describe your body language as well as your words.

Bobby and Jake are both fans of music videos and get together daily to watch their favorite ones. Bobby tells Jake that he would do anything to look as cool as their favorite performer. Jake tells Bobby that the videos are not necessarily real and that the performers' lifestyles and bodies are not typical of students their age. One day after school Bobby tells Jake that getting a tattoo like their favorite star would be really cool. Jake knows he's not ready to change the way he looks right now.

1. Say no. How would Jake say no to Bobby?

____

____

2. Offer an alternative. What else could Jake do with Bobby that shows appreciation for their favorite star?

____

____

3. Stand your ground. What should Jake do if Bobby kept pressuring?

____

____

4. Walk away. Describe how Jake should get out of the situation.

____

____

5. Plan ahead. What could Jake do to avoid this situation? Who can help Jake practice refusing this action?

____

____

6. Have a support system. Who will stand by Jake and how can Jake best use their support?

____

____

Refusal Skills

Lesson: Building Self-Esteem

Some people think that you have no control over your own destiny. In fact, you do have some control over how you feel about yourself and about the positive and negative things that happen in your life. Respecting yourself, your personal integrity, knowing and accepting yourself, setting goals, and being positive are all strategies to develop healthy self-esteem.

Read the following scenarios and take control of the situations using refusal skills.

1. Your friends want you to go into an Internet chat room and vandalize the chat. What do you do?

____

____

____

____

2. One of your friends seems to get everything he wants by getting angry at his family and harassing them until they give in. He wants you to manipulate your family to get things you know you really don't need. How do you answer him?

____

____

____

____

3. You told a white lie to impress a bunch of classmates you don't really hang out with. You said you had shoplifted a candy bar at the local convenience store. You would never do such a thing, but now these people want you to do it again while they watch through the window of the store. How do you say no?

____

____

____

____

Decision-Making Skills

Lesson: Your Self-Concept

Read the following situation. Then, follow the steps below to decide what you would do in this situation.

Jennifer and Ken are at the school dance and decide to head outside to get some air. A group of people have already gathered outside. Within a few minutes, someone pulls out a pack of cigarettes and begins passing it around. When the pack gets to Jennifer, she takes one and then hands the pack to Ken. Ken is adamantly against smoking. Ken holds the pack out to Jennifer, gesturing for her to put her cigarette back in the pack.

1. Identify the problem. What decision does Jennifer have to make?

____

____

2. Consider your values. What is important to Jennifer?

____

____

3. List the options. What possible actions could Jennifer take?

____

____

4. Weigh the consequences. List the pros and cons of each option.

____

____

5. Decide and act. Describe what Jennifer will do. Explain her decision.

____

____

6. Evaluate your choice. How do you feel about the action Jennifer took? Did she make a good decision? Would she take a different action if faced with the same scenario again?

____

____

Decision-Making Skills

Lesson: Building Self-Esteem

Read the following situation. Then, in the space below, explain how you would use decision-making skills if you were in Marshall's position.

Manny and Marshall are walking home from the food mart when they see the neighborhood bully picking on their friend's little brother, Pedro. Manny says to Marshall, "Let's go beat the trash out of that thug." Marshall knows bullies have low self-esteem, and that challenging a bully will only demonstrate Marshall's and Manny's own lack of self-esteem. So Marshall walks over to Pedro and stands between Pedro and the bully. Marshall says that Pedro needs to go home right away and that he and Manny are there to make sure Pedro gets home. As they turn to leave, the bully challenges Marshall.

____

____

____

____

____

____

____

____

____

____

____

____

____

____

____

Cross-Disciplinary: Language Arts

Lesson: Your Self-Concept

In groups of five, create a short play using one of the four ideas provided below. In the play, every person in the group must play a part. Groups should use the idea they choose only as a foundation for the play. More than one group can select the same idea.

Lead #1. Your favorite music star is reported to be suffering from anorexia nervosa.

Lead #2. Your favorite actor is arrested for underaged drinking while leaving a club with a group of friends.

Lead #3. A popular student at your school is recognized for volunteering at a soup kitchen for the homeless.

Lead #4. A good friend is being criticized for speaking out over a student being bullied after school in the parking lot.

Cross-Disciplinary: Art

Lesson: Self-Esteem and You

In groups of five, design a short music video which emphasizes how to build more healthy self-esteem. The music video can use pre-recorded music or you can create your own. In the boxes below, storyboard the scenes that will need to be shot for the video. Storyboarding is how movie producers lay out the sequence of events that will be filmed, almost like the newspaper comics. Use the boxes to create the storyline for your music video, in pictures. The storyboards need not be elaborate art but rather descriptive drawings that may require written explanations at the bottom. For example, the picture may show someone helping another person, with the explanation "helps person across street" written at the bottom.

Quiz

Lesson: Self-Esteem and You

Write the letter of the correct answer in the space provided.

_______ **1.** A measure of how much you value, respect, and feel confident about yourself is
- **a.** self-concept.
- **b.** body image.
- **c.** self-esteem.
- **d.** self–motivation.

_______ **2.** Identify the factor(s) which can influence self-esteem.
- **a.** friends
- **b.** family
- **c.** teachers
- **d.** All of the above

_______ **3.** The person who influences your self-esteem the most is
- **a.** you.
- **b.** coaches.
- **c.** media.
- **d.** teachers.

_______ **4.** Which of the following are characteristics of people who have high self-esteem?
- **a.** They do not like themselves.
- **b.** They know their strengths and weaknesses.
- **c.** They cannot accept who they are.
- **d.** They do not feel good about themselves.

_______ **5.** Which of the following are characteristics of people who have low self-esteem?
- **a.** They like their physical appearance.
- **b.** They practice healthy behaviors.
- **c.** They are affected deeply by what others say about them.
- **d.** None of the above

Quiz

Lesson: Your Self-Concept

Write the letter of the correct answer in the space provided.

_______ **1.** The way you see yourself in comparison to other people is called
- **a.** self-concept.
- **b.** body image.
- **c.** self-esteem.
- **d.** self–motivation.

_______ **2.** From which areas does your overall self-concept develop?
- **a.** academic self-concept
- **b.** physical self-concept
- **c.** social self-concept
- **d.** All of the above

_______ **3.** How you see your physical abilities is your
- **a.** academic self-concept.
- **b.** physical self-concept.
- **c.** social self-concept.
- **d.** All of the above

Match the definitions with the correct term. Write the letter of the correct answer in the space provided.

_______ **4.** seeing yourself as a very good friend

_______ **5.** seeing yourself as a student

_______ **6.** seeing yourself as an average athlete

_______ **7.** can help build self-esteem

_______ **8.** seeing yourself as a very good athlete

a. self-concept

b. physical self-concept

c. academic self-concept

d. social self-concept

Assessment

Quiz

Lesson: Building Self-Esteem

Write the letter of the correct answer in the space provided.

_______ **1.** By having integrity, respecting yourself, and being assertive you can build
  a. self-concept.
  b. body image.
  c. self-motivation.
  d. good character.

_______ **2.** The ability to take responsibility for your actions is called
  a. academic self-concept.
  b. physical self-concept.
  c. integrity.
  d. All of the above

_______ **3.** Acting on your values in an honest and respectful way is called
  a. integrity.
  b. respecting yourself.
  c. being assertive.
  d. All of the above

Match the definitions with the correct term. Write the letter of the correct answer in the space provided. Some terms will not be used.

_______ **4.** volunteering

_______ **5.** dealing with disappointment in a positive way

_______ **6.** being your own personal cheerleader

_______ **7.** knowing your strengths

a. get to know yourself

b. accept yourself

c. be good at something

d. set a goal

e. be positive

f. turn problems into challenges

g. do something for others

Chapter Test

Self-Esteem
USING VOCABULARY

Use the terms from the following list to complete the sentences. Each term may only be used once. Some terms will not be used.

family   self-concept
social self-concept   media
physical self-concept   being assertive
self-esteem   body image
academic self-concept   integrity

1. The measure of how much you value, respect, and feel confident about

yourself is your ____________________.

2. Your ability to take responsibility for your actions is your

____________________.

3. The area of your personality called ____________________ describes the

way you see yourself in comparison to your classmates.

4. The media can influence your ____________________ by only showing

people who are very successful and unusually attractive.

5. The way you imagine yourself as a person is your ____________________.

6. Your ____________________ is how you see your physical abilities.

UNDERSTANDING CONCEPTS

_______ **7.** Which of the following is a way to build healthy self-esteem?
     a. integrity
     b. respecting yourself
     c. being assertive
     d. All of the above

_______ **8.** Which area of self-concept addresses how you see yourself as a
student?
     a. academic self-concept
     b. physical self-concept
     c. social self-concept
     d. emotional self-concept

| Chapter Test *continued*

_______ **9.** Which of the following is NOT considered an influence on your
self-esteem?
  a. family
  b. peers
  c. popularity
  d. teachers

_______ **10.** How much you like yourself as a person is called your
  a. self-concept.
  b. self-esteem.
  c. body image.
  d. self-awareness.

_______ **11.** How much you value yourself and how you feel about yourself is
called your
  a. self-concept.
  b. self-esteem.
  c. body image.
  d. self-awareness.

12. List seven ways to improve your self-esteem.

____

____

____

____

____

____

13. The number of students suffering from anorexia nervosa and bulimia nervosa
in an attempt to control their body image has increased significantly over the
past couple of years. In media advertisements, TV shows, and music videos,
characters who are very thin and have very athletic bodies wear the latest
fashions, and drive the coolest cars. What would you say to a friend who said
to you, "I would do anything to be like them"?

____

____

____

____

14. Why does doing something for others build healthy self-esteem? What would you say to a friend who thought it was strange for you to suggest that you both volunteer your time to help homeless people?

____

____

____

____

CRITICAL THINKING

15. Marisa gets together every week with a group of friends who watch their favorite television show. The group of six girls are really into the characters. So much so that two of Marisa's friends are starting to worry her. Julie wants to be as popular as her favorite character and is starting to take risks to make herself look more mature. Lisa, who is a really smart and nice person, thinks she is too heavy. Lisa is considering taking diet pills like her favorite character on the show does. Marisa thinks she's okay, but she wants her brother to wear designer clothes and get a more fashionable haircut, to look like her favorite male character from the show. What should Marisa tell her friends? What should they tell her?

____

____

____

____

16. Asking questions and trying new things are ways to get to know yourself better. What questions should you ask yourself to get a better handle on who you are and to answer the question, "Do you have healthy self-esteem?"

____

____

____

____

Chapter Test *continued*

CONCEPT MAPPING

17. Use the following terms to complete the concept map below: *family, grow, friends, self-esteem, teachers, coaches,* and *influenced.*

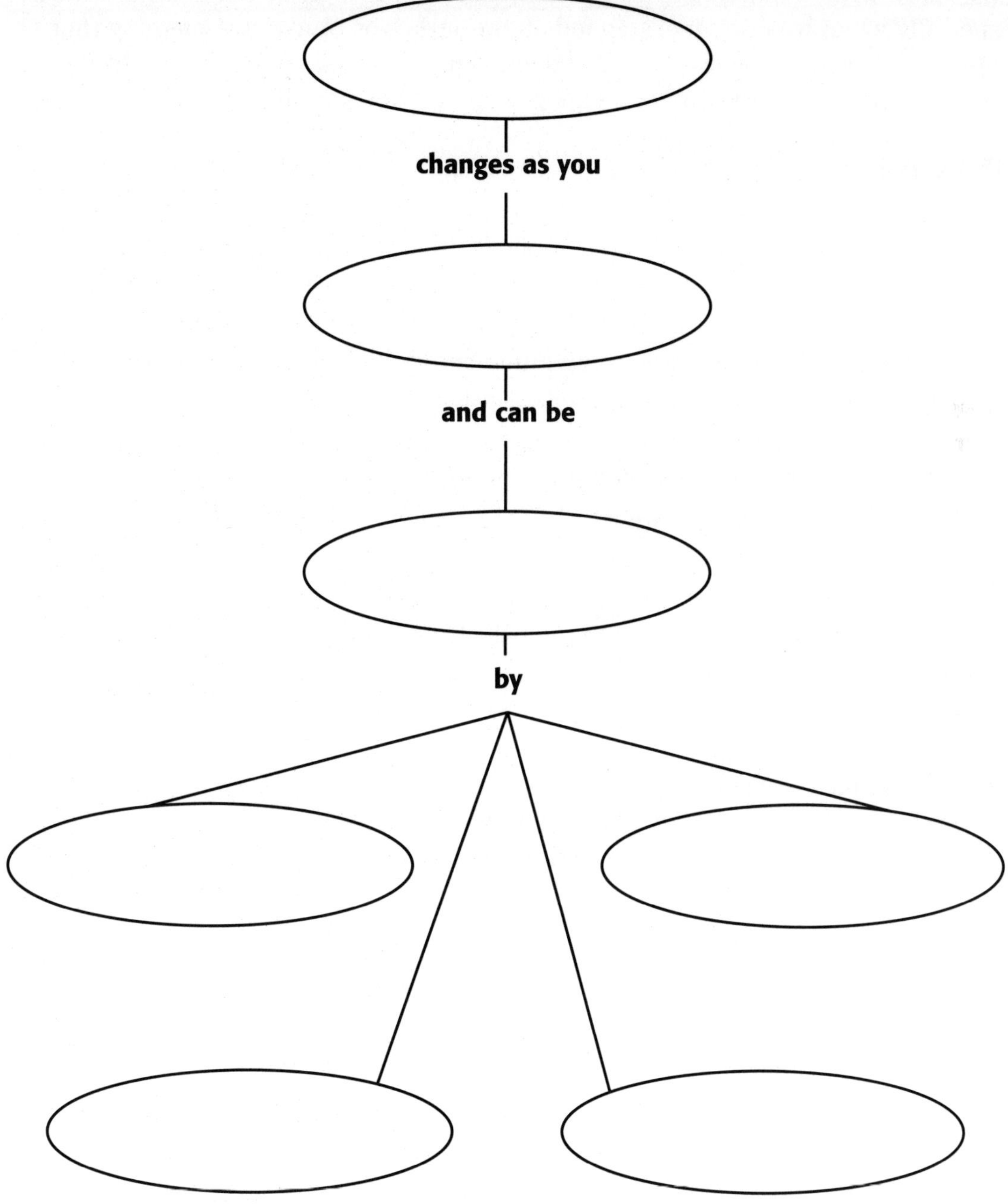

Performance-Based Assessment

Boosting Self-Esteem

INTRODUCTION

Self-esteem is the foundation of our personality. Building healthy self-esteem takes hard work. Sometimes our self-esteem is not as high as it is at other times, especially when we don't feel so good about ourselves or about something that happened. However, when our self-esteem is high we feel good about ourselves. This assessment will explore one experience that boosts self-esteem.

OBJECTIVE

- Keep in mind that your teachers will be observing and grading your in-class behavior as well as your written responses. In particular, your teacher will be noting your ability to follow the given procedures, how well you follow classroom safety guidelines, and your methods and reasoning in solving problems.

- Try not to let what others are doing influence your work. Remember that a problem often has several acceptable solutions.

- Do not talk to other students unless you are working in a group. Talk only to members of your group and try not to disturb other students.

- Use only the materials provided.

MATERIALS AND EQUIPMENT

- An award that you have earned previously. If you have not had the opportunity to win an award, tell your teacher.

PROCEDURE

1. You may have some type of award you received for an activity you participated in. It may be a plaque for an academic accomplishment, a trophy for some athletic accomplishment, a certificate for participation in an event, or a medallion for completing a task. Choose the one award which means the most to you. It may not be the largest, prettiest, or most impressive looking of your awards, but it gives you the greatest sense of pride over all the others. Which award did you choose?

____

____

____

____

Performance-Based Assessment *continued*

2. Write a paragraph about the circumstances that surrounded your receiving the award. Use the following questions to help you write your paragraph. How long did you have to work to get it? How much time did it take to prepare yourself for the task? What kind of effort did you have to produce to accomplish the task? What other people assisted you in accomplishing the task? Who else was competing for the award? How were you presented the award? Who else expressed pride in your receiving the award?

3. Take the circumstances you identified previously and write a 20-second introduction for your award. Be specific and to the point because someone else is going to read it to the class.

4. Bring your award and the introduction you wrote to class.

ANALYSIS

5. From your experience, and from watching your classmates present their awards, do the largest awards always provide the most self-esteem? Explain your answer.

____

____

____

____

6. Your level of self-esteem affects your success at most everything you do. How would providing awards to people impact their level of success?

____

____

____

____

7. What are some ideas for improving the self-esteem of your classmates?

____

____

____

____

Datasheet for In-Text Activity

Sell Yourself!

1. Make a list of your likes and dislikes. Then, make a list of your strengths. Finally, make a list of your weaknesses that you would like to improve.

Likes

1. _____________________
2. _____________________
3. _____________________
4. _____________________
5. _____________________

Dislikes

1. _____________________
2. _____________________
3. _____________________
4. _____________________
5. _____________________

Strengths

1. _____________________
2. _____________________
3. _____________________
4. _____________________
5. _____________________

Weaknesses

1. _____________________
2. _____________________
3. _____________________
4. _____________________
5. _____________________

Datasheet for In-Text Activity *continued*

2. Using your lists, posterboard, markers, construction paper, and magazine cutouts, create a billboard that describes you. Use the billboard to advertise yourself.

____

____

____

____

3. Create a commercial using your billboard, and present your commercial to the class.

____

____

____

____

ANALYSIS

1. What did you use to describe your strengths? Was it hard to describe the weaknesses you wanted to improve?

____

____

____

2. After creating your billboard and commercial, do you feel more confident about yourself? Explain your answer.

____

____

____

Life Skills: Communicating Effectively

Lesson: Self-Esteem and You

SELF-TALK: COMMUNICATING WITH YOURSELF

1. Situations often arise that make us feel stupid or clumsy. It may be that we dropped our books in the hallway, tripped going up the steps, or had some of this morning's breakfast still in our teeth. Situations like these happen to everyone at one time or another. Regardless, we still feel embarrassed. Identify your most recent embarrassing moment.

____

____

____

2. When this embarrassing situation happened, what did you say to yourself? Many times people are really hard on themselves saying things like, "You dummy," "What an idiot I am," and "I am such a freak." Negative self-talk lowers our level of self-esteem. What if we responded by laughing at the situation and talking to ourselves in a positive way? Describe how you could have reacted to your most recent embarrassing moment using positive self-talk.

____

____

____

Write down a positive response to the potentially embarrassing situations presented below.

1. You trip going up the steps.

____

____

2. You discover part of your lunch in your teeth.

____

____

3. You drop your books in the hall.

____

____

 Activity)

Life Skills: Setting Goals

Lesson: Building Self-Esteem
SETTING GOALS TO GUIDE US

If you do not know where you're going, any road will take you there. You may have heard this before. It not only applies to a journey in the car, but to your quest for success as well. It has been said that "life is a journey," so if you want to achieve certain goals, then you must plan your trip. You may want to be a star athlete, an excellent student, or a terrific musician. To achieve these goals, you must plan your journey. First of all, you need to decide a few things.

In the space provided answer the questions about your "journey."

1. As the old saying goes, "What do you want to be when you grow up?"

____

____

2. Identify three people who currently have the kind of position you identified above. They can be people you know, people you have seen in the media, or someone you have only heard about.

____

____

____

3. List three characteristics that each of the people listed above have. Such characteristics might include being funny, honest, trusting, loving, or any other characteristic. If you're not sure, then identify characteristics you feel they probably have.

a1 _______________   b1 _______________   c1 _______________

a2 _______________   b2 _______________   c2 _______________

a3 _______________   b3 _______________   c3 _______________

4. Which characteristics did any of the people share?

____

____

____

Life Skills: Setting Goals *continued*

5. Are all the characteristics listed important to developing positive self-esteem? Place a check mark next to the characteristics in question 3 that help develop positive self-esteem. Place an *X* next to the characteristics in question 3 that you think you currently have.

6. Explain why you think that you have the characteristics you placed an *X* next to.

____

____

____

7. Write down ways you could develop the characteristics you did not place an *X* next to (hint: the seven ways to healthy self-esteem may be helpful).

____

____

____

____

____

____

8. Describe how these characteristics would help you along the road to success.

____

____

____

____

Enrichment Activity

Lesson: Self-Esteem and You

Typically, successful people have healthy self-esteem. However, successful people also realize that maintaining their healthy self-esteem requires diligence and continued improvement. It was once said that someone who doesn't read is no better than someone who can't.

In this activity you will be asked to identify a book on a topic that could inspire healthy self-esteem. It can be a book based on a personal story of achievement, a motivational book, or a book on self-improvement. Once you have identified your book and are ready to start reading, have a pen and some 4x6 notecards at your side. While you're reading, when you come across a meaningful quote, write it on one of the cards. Write in large print so that the saying fills the entire front of the card. On the back, write the title of the book and the author, in the lower right corner. You should have between 15 and 20 cards by the book's end.

Your cards can serve many purposes. They can be used to insert quotes in to writing for other classes; they can be used to make a poster of self-esteem for your bedroom wall. They can be valuable in preparing a media presentation, and, by reviewing them monthly, they can be simply inspirational.

Write your three favorite sayings from your cards.

____

____

____

____

____

____

____

____

____

____

____

____

Name _____________________________________ Class _______________ Date _______________

Enrichment Activity

Lesson: Your Self-Concept

Success leaves clues. Successful people have a positive self-concept developed over years of achieving and failing. In trying to develop a more positive self-concept, it can be valuable to discover how other people who are currently successful developed and maintained their positive self-concept.

For this activity, identify five community leaders who you believe are successful. It could be a politician, a business leader, a member of the clergy, or an athletic coach. Choose people who are at the top of their profession. Write each of them a letter (use the same letter for all five). In the letter, identify yourself as a student and inform them that this is a project on self-esteem for your class. Ask them if they would please answer the following questions: Do you believe having a positive self-concept helped you become successful? What activities do you participate in that help you maintain your positive self-concept? At what times do you feel your self-concept is not so positive? What suggestions would you make to promote a positive self-concept?

Include a stamped, self-addressed envelope with your letter to improve the chances of receiving a quick response. List your five successful people with their mailing addresses below. If they have an e-mail address, send two of the people your letter via e-mail.

1. ____

____

2. ____

____

3. ____

____

4. ____

____

5. ____

____

Activity

Enrichment Activity

Lesson: Building Self-Esteem

One of the best ways to learn is to teach. Develop a 15-minute lesson on self-esteem that you will teach to a third-grade class. To develop your lesson, decide on one concept (important idea) you want them to remember from your lesson. The concept could be, for example, "Healthy self-esteem means respecting yourself, "or "Being assertive builds self-esteem."

Storytelling is one of the best teaching techniques for this age group, so write a story about how some fictional characters developed healthy self-esteem by respecting themselves. At the end of your story list three to five questions for the students to answer out loud. Base your questions on the concept you wanted them to learn. Using the first example above, you may want to ask if they liked the story, if the characters respected themselves in the story, or how might the characters learn to respect themselves more.

Identify the concept you want the third grade to students learn.

____

On a separate sheet of paper, write your story.

List the three to five questions to ask the students after your story.

1. ____

____

2. ____

____

3. ____

____

4. ____

____

5. ____

____

Name _______________________________ Class _______________ Date _____________

Health Inventory

Self-Esteem

Use the following questions to help you evaluate your level of self-esteem.

yes	no		
❑	❑	**1.** I value, respect, and feel confident about myself.	40 points
❑	❑	**2.** I like the way I look.	15 points
❑	❑	**3.** I am comfortable with my body weight.	10 points
❑	❑	**4.** My friends are very supportive of me.	8 points
❑	❑	**5.** I rarely get upset with members of my family.	5 points
❑	❑	**6.** I am comfortable with my strengths and weaknesses and feel positive about myself, most of the time.	5 points
❑	❑	**7.** I see my body as normal and I am comfortable with it.	8 points
❑	❑	**8.** I see myself being exceptional at something some day.	5 points
❑	❑	**9.** As I grow emotionally, my self-concept will evolve.	3 points
❑	❑	**10.** I know that I must work at improving my self-esteem.	10 points

Add up the points for all of the questions to which you answered yes. Write your score here _______________.

Look at the scale to see how your level of self-esteem matches up. Remember, a scale like this is only one way to evaluate your level of self-esteem, so do not put a great deal of emphasis on a single measure.

40–109 points: You are the most comfortable with who you are and where you are going. Keep up the great work.

20–39 points: You feel pretty good about yourself but you still have some negative, stressful times

15-19 points: You are balancing between positive self-esteem and not so positive self-esteem. Look for more positive opportunities.

0-14 points: Your self-esteem appears low and could use a big boost.

Health Behavior Contract

Self-Esteem

My goals: I, _________________________________, will accomplish one or more of the following goals:

I will build a higher self-esteem.

I will focus on my strengths.

I will make a plan to improve my weaknesses.

Other: ____

____

My reasons: By building healthy self-esteem, I will improve my overall confidence and attitude, and I will feel good about myself as a person.

Other: ____

____

My values: Personal values that will help me meet my goals are

____

____

____

My plan: The actions I will take to meet my goals are

____

____

____

Evaluation: I will use my Health Journal to keep a log of actions I took to fulfill this contract. After one month, I will evaluate my goals. I will adjust my plan if my goals are not being met. If my goals are being met, I will consider setting additional goals.

Signed ____

Date ____

Activity)

At-Home Activity

Self-Esteem and the Media

Identify a magazine targeted at parents and a magazine targeted at teens. Search through both magazines and find an advertisement for items such as clothing, snacks, or cosmetic products. Also note advertisements which may be in one magazine but not in the other. Analyze the difference with a parent. Answer the following questions.

1. Were there any differences in the ads for similar products from one magazine to the other? Explain your answer.

____

____

2. How did the ads for clothing differ from one magazine to the other?

____

____

3. Are advertisers using models with the same type of body in both magazines?

____

____

4. Do you think the magazine advertisements promote a positive body image? Why or why not?

____

____

The signatures below verify that our discussion has take place.

____

Student Signature   Class Period

____

Parent or Guardian Signature   Date

Name _________________________________ Class _____________ Date ____________

Actividad En Casa

La autoestima

Identifique una revista dirigida a los adultos y otra dirigida a los adolescentes. Busque en las dos revistas un anuncio comercial por algo como prendas de vertir, bocaditos, el maquillaje, etc. También, note los anuncios que están en una de las revistas pero no en la otra. Analice las diferencias con su padre/madre/tutor. Conteste las preguntas siguientes.

1. ¿Había diferencias entre las dos revistas en la propaganda por productos semejantes? Explique su respuesta.

____

____

2. ¿Cuáles eran las diferencias en los anuncios por ropa entre las dos revistas?

____

____

3. ¿Tienen los/las modelos la misma forma de cuerpo en las dos revistas? ¿Es una estrategia de los directores de publicidad? Explique.

____

____

4. A su parecer, ¿favorecen los anuncios de revista una imagen positiva del cuerpo? ¿Por qué sí o no?

____

____

Las firmas verifican que discutimos esta actividad juntos.

____

Firma de Estudiante   Período de Clase(la Salud)

____

Firma de Padre/Madre/Tutor   Fecha

Lesson Plan

Lesson: Self-Esteem and You

Pacing

45 minutes

Objectives

1. Explain how self-esteem affects your life.

2. Identify the characteristics of high self-esteem and low self-esteem.

3. Identify five influences on self-esteem.

Standards Covered

1.2 Describe the interrelationship of mental, emotional, social, and physical health during adolescence.

1.4 Describe how family and peers influence the health of adolescents.

4.2 Analyze how messages from media and other sources influence health behaviors.

KEY

SE = Student Edition   **ATE** = Annotated Teacher Edition

CRF = Chapter Resource File

CHAPTER OPENER

❏ **Health IQ, SE** To assess student knowledge of self-esteem, have students answer the Health IQ questions. Answers are at the bottom of the test.

FOCUS

❏ **Bellringer, ATE** Have students write a short paragraph describing some event or activity, that made them feel good about themselves.

❏ **Bellringer Transparency** Use this transparency as students enter the classroom and find their seats.

❏ **Start Off Write, SE** Ask students to write an answer to the following question: "How can your peers affect your self-esteem?"

MOTIVATE

❏ **Group Activity, What Is Self-Esteem?, ATE** Groups decide on the best definition for self-esteem and write it down. They make two lists: the characteristics of people with high self-esteem, and the characteristics of people with low self-esteem. **[GENERAL]**

Lesson Plan *continued*

TEACH

☐ **Life Skills Activity, Setting Goals, SE** Have the students write one thing they want to learn to do, but are afraid to try. Identify three things they can do to get started. Have them set a timeline to achieve their goal.

☐ **Activity, Dealing With Negative Comments, ATE** Students identify several strategies to deal with negative comments in a positive way, and list them on an index card. [GENERAL]

☐ **Life Skill Builder Evaluating Media Messages, ATE** Students list characteristics of people depicted in magazines and newspaper ads and compare to a list of characteristics for an average American. Students hunt for images of an average American. [GENERAL]

☐ **Teaching Transparency The Media and Your Self-Esteem** Use this graphic to help students understand self-esteem.

CLOSE

☐ **Lesson Quiz, ATE** Students answer 3 questions about self-esteem. [GENERAL]

☐ **Lesson Quiz, CRF** Students answer 10 questions about self-esteem. [GENERAL]

☐ **Concept Review, CRF** These questions will support material from lesson. [GENERAL]

HOMEWORK

☐ **Lesson Review, SE** Assign questions 1–4 for review, homework, or quiz.

OTHER RESOURCE OPTIONS

☐ **Reading Skill Builder Anticipation Guide, ATE** Students to predict who affects their self-esteem prior to reading the text. [GENERAL]

☐ **Guided Audio CD Program, Self-Esteem.** The audio program is a reading of the chapter content for ELL students, auditory learners, and struggling readers.

☐ **Discussion: Too Much Self-Esteem? ATE** Ask students to describe someone who they felt had too much self-esteem. [GENERAL]

☐ **Directed Reading, CRF** Have students answer questions as they read the lesson. [BASIC]

☐ **Enrichment Activity, CRF** Students are asked to read an inspirational book and generate quotes on 3x5 cards. [ADVANCED]

☐ **go.hrw.com** For worksheets, videos, and other teaching aids related to this chapter, visit the HRW Web site and type in the keyword HD4SE6.

☐ **VideoSelect** Videos related to the chapter may be found at go.hrw.com. Type in the keyword HD4SE6V.

Lesson Plan

Lesson: Your Self-Concept

Pacing

15 Minutes

Objectives

1. Describe how self-concept and self-esteem are different.

2. Identify three areas of self-concept.

Standards Covered

1.2 Describe the interrelationship of mental, emotional, social, and physical health during adolescence.

> **KEY**
> **SE** = Student Edition **ATE** = Annotated Teacher Edition
> **CRF** = Chapter Resource File

FOCUS

❏ **Bellringer, ATE** Have students describe their favorite school subject and explain why it's their favorite.

❏ **Bellringer Transparency** Use this transparency as students enter the classroom and find their seats.

❏ **Start Off Write, SE** Ask students to write an answer to the following question: "How does self-concept develop?"

MOTIVATE

❏ **Demonstration, Self-Esteem and Self-Concept, ATE** Explain the connection between self-esteem and the factors which contribute to it by drawing an illustration on the board. **[GENERAL]**

TEACH

❏ **Activity, Poster Project, ATE** Have students draw, paint, or make a collage with magazine clippings of how they see themselves academically, physically, and socially. **[BASIC]**

❏ **Refusal Skills, CRF** Students respond to a story which places one of the characters in a situation about self-concept and pressure to do drugs. **[GENERAL]**

❏ **Inclusion Strategies, ATE** Students interview people about their self-concept. **[ADVANCED]**

Lesson Plan *continued*

CLOSE

❏ **Lesson Quiz, ATE** Students respond to 7 sentences about self-concept.

❏ **Lesson Quiz, CRF** Students answer 10 questions about self-concept.
[GENERAL]

❏ **Concept Review, CRF** This exercise reinforces the material covered in the lesson. [GENERAL]

HOMEWORK

❏ **Lesson Review, SE** Assign questions 1–5 for review, homework or quiz.

❏ **Concept Mapping, CRF** Have students complete the concept map about self-esteem and self-concept. [GENERAL]

OTHER RESOURCE OPTIONS

❏ **Directed Reading, CRF** Students answer questions as they read the lesson.
[BASIC]

❏ **Decision-Making Skills, CRF** Have students complete the questions after reading the story about peer pressure to smoke. [GENERAL]

❏ **Enrichment Activity, CRF** Students write letters to community leaders asking them to answer questions about self-esteem. [ADVANCED]

❏ **Guided Audio CD Program, Self-Esteem.** The audio program is a reading of the chapter content for ELL students, auditory learners, and struggling readers.

❏ **go.hrw.com** For worksheets, videos, and other teaching aids related to this chapter, visit the HRW Web site and type in the keyword HD4SE6.

❏ **VideoSelect** Videos related to the chapter may be found at go.hrw.com. Type in the keyword HD4SE6V.

Lesson Plan

Lesson: Building Self-Esteem

Pacing

30 Minutes

Objectives

1. Identify three keys to healthy self-esteem.

2. Identify seven ways to build healthy self-esteem.

Standards Covered

1.2 Describe the interrelationship of mental, emotional, social, and physical health during adolescence

3.4 Demonstrate strategies to improve or maintain personal and family health.

6.4 Apply strategies and skills needed to attain personal health goals

---

KEY

SE = Student Edition   **ATE** = Annotated Teacher Edition

CRF = Chapter Resource File

FOCUS

❑ **Bellringer, ATE** Ask students what it means to have self-respect.

❑ **Bellringer Transparency** Use this transparency as students enter the classroom and find their seats.

❑ **Start Off Write, SE** Ask students to write an answer to the following question: "What can you do to build healthy self-esteem?"

MOTIVATE

❑ **Debate, Honesty, ATE** Ask students whether they believe that the adage "honesty is the best policy," is true or not. **[GENERAL]**

TEACH

❑ **Enrichment Activity, CRF** Students identify a noteworthy concept from the lesson and prepare to teach a 15-minute lesson to third graders. **[GENERAL]**

❑ **Hands-On Activity: Sell Yourself, SE** Students list their likes and dislikes and their strengths and weaknesses thencreate a billboard to advertise themselves. **[GENERAL]**

❑ **Datasheet for In-Text Activity, Sell Yourself, CRF** Students use this worksheet to record data for the Hands-On Activity. **[BASIC]**

❑ **Inclusion Strategies, SE** Students create an idea map that outlines three keys to healthy self-esteem. **[BASIC]**

Lesson Plan *continued*

- **Reading SkillBuilder, Paired Summarizing, ATE** Have pairs of students silently read the text and then take turns summarizing the content. [GENERAL]
- **Activity, Hobbies, ATE** Have the students list five hobbies they enjoy. Then identify the last time they actually did the activity. Have them pick one to do this week. [GENERAL]

CLOSE

- **Lesson Quiz, ATE** Students answer 4 questions about self-esteem. [GENERAL]
- **Lesson Quiz, CRF** Students answer 9 questions about self-esteem. [GENERAL]
- **Concept Review, CRF** This exercise reinforces the material covered in lesson. [GENERAL]

HOMEWORK

- **Lesson Review, SE** Assign questions 1-4 for review, homework, or quiz.

OTHER RESOURCE OPTIONS

- **Life Skill Builder, Goal Setting, ATE** Students set a goal to organize their lockers or bedroom. Once a plan is made, "before" pictures are taken and after the plan has been implemented "after" pictures are taken. Students make a brochure using the pictures and identifying areas of greatest need. A paragraph describing how this experience made them feel is at the end of the brochure. [GENERAL]
- **Real Life Connection, Volunteer, ATE** Students volunteer to help a charity of their choice and write a paper describing the experience. [GENERAL]
- **Directed Reading, CRF** Students answer questions as they read the lesson. [BASIC]
- **Internet Connect** Building Healthy Self-Esteem, Healthlinks Code HD4020. Students research Internet sources about self-esteem.
- **go.hrw.com** For worksheets, videos, and other teaching aids related to this chapter, visit the HRW Web site and type in the keyword HD4SE6.
- **VideoSelect** Videos related to the chapter may be found at go.hrw.com. Type in the keyword HD4SE6V.
- **Guided Audio CD Program, Self-Esteem.** The audio program is a reading of the chapter content for ELL students, auditory learners, and struggling readers.

Lesson Plan

End of Chapter Review and Assessment

Pacing

90 minutes

> **KEY**
> **SE** = Student Edition   **ATE** = Annotated Teacher Edition
> **CRF** = Chapter Resource File

Review

- ❑ **Chapter Review, SE** Assign questions to review the material for this chapter. Use the assignment guide to customize review for lessons covered.

- ❑ **Concept Review, CRF** Vocabulary and concept review for each lesson [GENERAL]

Assessment

- ❑ **Chapter Test, Self-Esteem, CRF** Assign questions for general level chapter assessment. [GENERAL]

- ❑ **Performance-Based Assessment, Boosting Self-Esteem, CRF [GENERAL]**

- ❑ **Test Generator One-Stop Planner** Create a customized homework, quiz, or test using the HRW Test Generator program.

- ❑ **Test Item Listing, CRF** Use the Test Item Listing to identify questions for a customized homework, quiz, or test.

Parent Letter *6th grade*

Self-Esteem

Dear Parent or Guardian:

Self-esteem is one of those topics which has the potential to impact virtually every other aspect of your child's health. Low self-esteem can create a situation where success, academic as well as social, is difficult to achieve.

During the next couple of weeks your son or daughter will be learning about many factors that affect his or her self-esteem. We will be exploring the foundations of healthy self-esteem, how it is normal to have times when our self-esteem is high and other times when it is low and how other people can influence self-esteem both positively and negatively. Other topics that will be explored include the characteristics of people with high self-esteem, the definition of self-concept, the impact of media on body image, and ways to build healthy self-esteem.

Encourage your son or daughter to share what he or she has learned with you.

One way your son or daughter can share with you what he or she is learning in school is the At-Home Activity. The activity addresses the impact of advertisements on body image and self-esteem. This activity should not only be fun for both you and your child, but quite educational as well. Your signature on the bottom of the worksheet will indicate that your child has brought home the At-Home Activity and discussed it with you.

Thank you for your continued support and cooperation.

Sincerely,

____

Health Teacher

Carta a las Padres/al Tutor *6th grade*

La autoestima

Estimado(s) Padres/Tutor:

La autoestima es un tema que tiene la posibilidad de influir en casi todos los aspectos de la salud de su hijo/a. Poca autoestima puede crear una situación en la que el éxito, tanto académico como social, sea difícil de lograr.

Durante las próximas semanas, su hijo/a va a aprender de muchos factores que rigen su autoestima. Se estudiarán la base de una autoestima sana, lo normal que es tener épocas de mucha autoestima y otras de poca y el efecto positivo o negativo que otras personas pueden tener en ella.

Otros asuntos tratados son las característicaas de personas con mucha autoestima, lo que es el concepto de sí, la influencia de los medios de comunicación en la imagen personal del cuerpo y modos de fortalecer la autoestima sana.

Ud. puede ayudar a su hijo/a en esta clase por hablar con él o ella sobre los temas que estudie. Para facilitar esta comunicación le mando una hoja de trabajo, La autoestima, para completar con él/ella. La actividad se trata del impacto de los anuncios comericales en la imagen del cuerpo y la autoestima. Su firma en la hoja verifica que Uds. discutieron esta actividad juntos.

Gracias anticipadas por su tiempo, cooperación y apoyo.

Atentamente,

____

Maestro/a de Salud

Assessment

Performance-Based Assessment

Boosting Self-Esteem

Teacher's Notes

INTRODUCTION

Self-esteem is the foundation of our personality. Whenever we are recognized for something positive we accomplished, our level of self-esteem is high and we feel very proud. This assessment will explore one of those experiences.

TIME REQUIRED One 45-minute class period

P.B.A. RATINGS
Teacher Prep—1
Student Set-Up—1
Concept Level—2
Clean Up—1

Easy ← 1   2   3   4 → Hard

ADVANCE PREPARATION

Students will need to be reminded in advance to bring in their awards. Students will need 25 minutes to analyze and describe the award and to answer the analysis questions and 20 minutes to present all award descriptions.

Have available a bulletin board with a table underneath for the students to display their awards until the appropriate class time. Have blank award certificates handy for those students who may have never received an award. You can say a few positive comments about the student in place of the student's description of his or her award.

PERFORMANCE

At the end of the assessment, students should turn in the following items:

• The description of the award

• Worksheet with answers to Analysis questions

EVALUATION

The following is a recommended breakdown for evaluating student performance:
30%. Appropriate use of materials and equipment.
40%. Quality and accuracy of presentation.
30%. Analysis

Answer Key

Directed Reading

LESSON: SELF-ESTEEM AND YOU

1. self-esteem
2. A measure of how much you value, respect, and feel confident about yourself. Or, how much you like yourself.
3. d
4. feel good about themselves, know their strengths and weaknesses, accept who they are, and they like themselves
5. low
6. high
7. d
8. low self-esteem
9. c
10. self-esteem
11. family, friends, teachers, and or coaches
12. support
13. high
14. teasing or bullying
15. b
16. The media tends to show only people who are very successful and unusually attractive. Unrealistic expectations are believed to be achievable.
17. d
18. body image

LESSON: YOUR SELF-CONCEPT

19. self-concept
20. Self-concept is the way you imagine and see yourself as a person. Self-esteem is how you feel about yourself. Self-concept is a part of your self-esteem.
21. self-concept
22. self-esteem
23. positive
24. d
25. social
26. S
27. A
28. P
29. S
30. A
31. self-concept
32. self-esteem

LESSON: BUILDING SELF-ESTEEM

33. self-esteem
34. integrity, respecting yourself, and being assertive.
35. a
36. integrity
37. right; wrong
38. assertive
39. know yourself
40. accept yourself
41. getting to know yourself
42. doing something for others
43. being good at something
44. setting a goal

Concept Mapping

LESSON: SELF-ESTEEM AND YOU

Your *self-esteem* is a measure of how much you *value yourself, respect yourself,* and *feel confident about yourself,* and if you have *healthy* self-esteem, it will affect your success at *school, relationships,* and *facing new situations.*

LESSON: YOUR SELF-CONCEPT

Answers may vary. Sample answer: Your *self-esteem* is influenced by your *self-concept,* which has three parts— *academic,* which reflects how you see yourself as a *student, social,* which is how you are as a *friend* and in *relationships,* and *physical,* which may include how you see yourself as an *athlete.*

Concept Review

LESSON: SELF-ESTEEM AND YOU

1. HSE
2. HSE
3. LSE
4. HSE
5. HSE
6. HSE
7. LSE
8. HSE
9. HSE

10. HSE

11. Answers may vary. Sample answers: Displaying body images which are not typical can lead to frustration resulting in a lower self-esteem because of an inability to achieve such an ideal body image.

12. body image

LESSON: YOUR SELF-CONCEPT

13. self-esteem
14. self-concept
15. academic self-concept
16. physical self-concept
17. social self-concept
18. negative
19. SS
20. AS
21. PS
22. SS
23. SS

LESSON: BUILDING SELF-ESTEEM

24. integrity, respecting yourself, being assertive
25. integrity
26. being assertive
27. respecting
28. strengths/weaknesses
29. volunteering
30. Answers may vary. Sample answers: get to know yourself, accept yourself, be good at something, set a goal, be positive, turn problems into challenges, do something for others.
31. accepting
32. setting
33. being positive

Refusal Skills

LESSON: YOUR SELF-CONCEPT

Answers may vary. Sample answers:
1. "I am not interested in a tattoo."
2. "Lets go check out the new music videos."
3. "I've got to be somewhere soon, I don't have time."
4. Look at the time. I have got to go, now."
5. Make it clear that a tattoo is out of the question because if your coach found out he would tell your parents.
6. parents and friends can be of great support.

LESSON: BUILDING SELF-ESTEEM

Answers may vary. Sample answers:
1. Refuse to interrupt the Internet chat. Suggest some other constructive internet activity. Get support from other friends.
2. Tell your friend your family does not respond to anger or harassment. An alternative would be to do some chores in exchange for what you want. Ask other friends how their families deal with their requests.
3. Say you thought about it and you don't ever want to take the risk of shoplifting. Walk away and decide that these are not the kind of kids you should spend time with.

Decision-Making Skills

LESSON: YOUR SELF-CONCEPT

Answers may vary. Sample answers:
1. To smoke or not
2. Staying healthy, having friends
3. Replace the cigarette in the pack or light up with the others
4. If she replaces the cigarette, she will not do anything harmful to her health and she will have Ken's respect. If she smokes, she will be hurting her health and losing Ken's respect, though the others may approve.
5. She decides not to smoke the cigarette. She agrees with Ken, though she felt some pressure from others. She realized Ken had her best interests in mind and that the others aren't really friends if they wanted her to do something unhealthy.
6. She made a good choice. She might have made a different decision if Ken hadn't been there to influence her.

LESSON: BUILDING SELF-ESTEEM

Answers may vary. Students should explain how to deal with the bully. Simply walk away, tell the bully you're not a worthy opponent, etc.

Cross-Disciplinary: Language Arts

LESSON: YOUR SELF-CONCEPT

Answers may vary, each should discuss how integrity, respecting yourself, and being assertive builds character which impacts healthy self-esteem.

Cross-Disciplinary: Art

LESSON: SELF-ESTEEM AND YOU

Answers may vary. Each music video or storyboard should address some area of self-esteem, body image, and/or self-concept.

Quiz

LESSON: SELF-ESTEEM AND YOU

1. c
2. d
3. a
4. b
5. c

LESSON: YOUR SELF-CONCEPT

1. a
2. d
3. b
4. d
5. c
6. b
7. a
8. b

LESSON: BUILDING SELF-ESTEEM

1. d
2. c
3. c
4. g
5. f
6. e
7. a

Chapter Test

SELF-ESTEEM

1. self-esteem
2. integrity
3. academic self-concept
4. body image
5. self-concept
6. physical self-concept

7. d
8. a
9. c
10. b
11. b
12. Get to know yourself, accept yourself, be good at something, set a goal, be positive, turn problems into challenges, and do something for others.
13. You would tell him or her that the media tends to show only people who are very successful and unusually attractive. A healthy self-esteem comes from having integrity, respecting yourself, and being assertive, not from trying to be like someone else.
14. Very few things make you feel as good as helping the who may be less fortunate. The increased confidence you will get from the little time you give will be well worth the boost to your self-esteem.
15. Answers may vary. Sample answer: Marisa should tellher friends to make healthy decisions rather than just imitating a TV character. They should remind her to let her brother make his own decisions.
16. Answers may vary. Sample answers: What kinds of things do I like to do? What kinds of things don't I like, what are my strengths, or positive qualities? What are my weaknesses?
17. *Self-esteem* changes as you *grow* and can be *influenced* by *family*, *friends*, *teachers*, and *coaches*.

Performance-Based Assessment

ANALYSIS

Answers may vary. Sample answers:

5. Size has little to do with the value of the award. Value is also quite personal. A small medallion from your church, for example, might be more meaningful than a large athletic trophy.
6. Being recognized by peers helps to build confidence, a fundamental building block of self-esteem. Having

a peer congratulate another peer provides for a discussion on the perception of recognition (provided by others) vs. arrogance (provided by self).

7. Some ideas may be to initiate an awards bulletin board for the students to maintain with classmates' awards. Students could also recognize other students for volunteer work they have done during the month.

Datasheet for In-Text Activity

LESSON: SELL YOURSELF!

Answers may vary. Sample answers:

1. I used magazine cutouts of paintings and art supplies, and I drew tennis rackets and tennis balls on my billboard because these are my strengths. Then, I used magazine cutouts of books on my billboard, because I feel that I could be better at reading. It wasn't very hard to describe my weaknesses with the pictures.
2. I feel more confident now because I will remember my strengths whenever I am feeling unsure of myself.

Life Skills: Communicating Effectively

LESSON: SELF-ESTEEM AND YOU

Answers may vary. Sample answers:

1. Note, the level of embarrassment will vary by student, time of year, and so forth.
2. Answers to the question which display positive self-talk in response to a potentially embarrassing situation are acceptable.
1. Any positive response is acceptable. For example, "Look back and laugh, or pretend to trip on the next three steps."
2. Any positive response is acceptable. For example, "Well that sure improved my looks."
3. Any positive response is acceptable. Sample answer: saying out loud, "OK, now jump back up," as if the books were a pet.

Life Skills: Setting Goals

LESSON: BUILDING SELF-ESTEEM

Answers may vary. Sample answers:

1. Any type of career goal is acceptable.
2. Three individuals should be identified.
3. Three characteristics per individual should be identified.
4. Any duplicate characteristics should be identified.
5. Students should have made the indications (check mark, X) next to the appropriate characteristic.
6. Accept any reasonable answer.
7. I would get better acquainted with myself and appreciate my strengths and I would accept the weaknesses too. I would pick something to get better at and set a goal. I would try to think positive and pat myself on the back. If I have a problem, I'll think of it as an opportunity. And I will volunteer to help others.
8. Discussion regarding goal setting and success would be appropriate here.

Enrichment Activities

LESSON: SELF-ESTEEM AND YOU

The cards the students generate will vary according to the book they read and the specific quotes of personal interest. The number of cards and the directions on how to write on the cards does not vary.

LESSON: YOUR SELF-CONCEPT

Answers may vary. Assistance in deciding where to send letters will be needed so that one individual does not receive multiple letters from the class. This can also be used as a technology class by using computers to locate mail and e-mail addresses.

LESSON: BUILDING SELF-ESTEEM

Answers may vary. The concepts the students will choose from can be taken directly from the opening page of each Lesson in the SE. Their stories can also be used as a cross-disciplinary activity by having the students use a specific theme for their stories. A third grade class is recommended, however, other grades are acceptable. Questions for the third graders should be very simple as suggested in the directions.

Health Inventory

Answers may vary. Assure students that the results of this inventory simply provide a "snapshot" of their self-esteem at that moment. This tool is best used to initiate discussion.

Health Behavior Contract

Answers may vary. Accept all reasonable answers.

At-Home Activity

Answers may vary. Sample answers:

1. This can be used to initiate a discussion on body image and maturity. The magazines geared for the younger population will typically use unusually attractive, young models with very slim figures. Magazines for parents will typically use more mature models engaging in a variety of activities.
2. The magazines geared for the younger population will typically show the latest fashions for teens. The parent magazines will typically show fashions more geared for the activity being highlighted.
3. The magazines geared for the younger population will typically use attractive, young models with very slim figures. Magazines for parents will vary depending on the activity being highlighted.
4. This can be used to initiate a discussion on body image and maturity. Because magazines geared for the younger population typically use unusually attractive, young models with very slim figures, unrealistic expectations are promoted.

Selected Spanish Answers

CONCEPT REVIEW

1. AEA
2. AEA
3. AEB
4. AEA
5. AEA
6. AEA
7. AEB
8. AEA
9. AEA
10. AEA

19. AS
20. AA
21. AF
22. AS
23. AS

31. ACEPTARTE
32. ESTABLECER
33. SER POSITIVO

Self-Esteem

MULTIPLE CHOICE

1. A person with healthy self-esteem would
   a. generally feel good about themselves.
   b. experience some low levels of self-esteem.
   c. be more likely to be successful.
   d. All of the above
   Answer: D   Difficulty: 1   Section: 1   Objective: 2

2. The person who influences your self-esteem the most is
   a. a family member.
   b. yourself.
   c. your friend.
   d. your teacher.
   Answer: B   Difficulty: 1   Section: 1   Objective: 2

3. Which of the following would be included in the media?
   a. television
   b. music videos
   c. movies
   d. All of the above
   Answer: D   Difficulty: 1   Section: 1   Objective: 3

4. Self-concept develops from which different areas of your personality?
   a. Academic self-concept
   b. Physical self-concept
   c. Social self-concept
   d. All of the above
   Answer: D   Difficulty: 1   Section: 2   Objective: 2

5 What is a positive way to build healthy self-esteem?
   a. respecting yourself
   b. being hard on yourself
   c. being aggressive
   d. being feared by others
   Answer: A   Difficulty: 1   Section: 3   Objective: 1

6. A measure of how much you value, respect, and feel confident about yourself is
   a. self-concept.
   b. body image.
   c. self-esteem.
   d. self–motivation.
   Answer: C   Difficulty: 1   Section: 1   Objective: 1

7. Identify the factor(s) which can influence self-esteem.
   a. friends
   b. family
   c. teachers
   d. All of the above
   Answer: D   Difficulty: 1   Section: 1   Objective: 2

8. Which of the following are characteristics of someone with high self-esteem?
   a. They do not like themselves.
   b. They know their strengths and weaknesses.
   c. They cannot accept who they are.
   d. They do not feel good about themselves.

   Answer: B   Difficulty: 1   Section: 1   Objective: 2

9. Which of the following are characteristics of someone with low self-esteem?
   a. They like their physical appearance.
   b. They practice healthy behaviors.
   c. They are affected deeply by what others say about them.
   d. None of the above

   Answer: C   Difficulty: 1   Section: 1   Objective: 2

10. The way you see yourself in comparison to other people is called
    a. self-concept.
    b. body image.
    c. self-esteem.
    d. self–motivation.

    Answer: A   Difficulty: 1   Section: 2   Objective: 1

11. In what area(s) of your personality does your self-concept originate?
    a. academic self-concept
    b. physical self-concept
    c. social self-concept
    d. All of the above

    Answer: D   Difficulty: 1   Section: 2   Objective: 2

12. How you see your physical abilities is your
    a. academic self-concept.
    b. physical self-concept.
    c. social self-concept.
    d. All of the above

    Answer: B   Difficulty: 1   Section: 2   Objective: 2

13. By having integrity, respecting yourself, and being assertive, you can build
    a. self-concept.
    b. body image.
    c. self-motivation.
    d. good character.

    Answer: D   Difficulty: 1   Section: 3   Objective: 1

14. The ability to take responsibility for your actions is
    a. academic self-concept.
    b. physical self-concept.
    c. integrity.
    d. All of the above

    Answer: C   Difficulty: 1   Section: 3   Objective: 1

15. Acting on your values in an honest and respectful way is
    a. integrity.
    b. respecting yourself.
    c. being assertive.
    d. All of the above

    Answer: C   Difficulty: 1   Section: 3   Objective: 1

16. Which is NOT one of the ways to build healthy self-esteem?
    a. intervention
    b. respecting yourself
    c. assertiveness
    d. integrity
    Answer: A   Difficulty: 1   Section: 3   Objective: 1

17. Which area of self-concept addresses how you see yourself as a student?
    a. academic self-concept
    b. physical self-concept
    c. social self-concept
    d. emotional self-concept
    Answer: A   Difficulty: 1   Section: 2   Objective: 2

18 Which of the following is NOT one of the five influences on your self-esteem?
    a. family
    b. peers
    c. animals
    d. teachers
    Answer: C   Difficulty: 1   Section: 1   Objective: 3

19. How much you like yourself as a person is called your
    a. self-concept.
    b. self-esteem.
    c. self-worth.
    d. self-awareness.
    Answer: B   Difficulty: 1   Section: 1   Objective: 1

20. How much you value yourself and how you feel about yourself is called your
    a. self-concept.
    b. self-esteem.
    c. self-worth.
    d. self-awareness.
    Answer: B   Difficulty: 1   Section: 1   Objective: 1

COMPLETION

21. Feeling good about yourself even when you may not be the best player at a particular
    sport or other activity is a sign of a healthy __________________.
    Answer: self-esteem   Difficulty: 1   Section: 1   Objective: 1

22. People with a __________________ self-esteem depend on other's opinions to
    determine how they feel about themselves.
    Answer: low   Difficulty: 1   Section: 1   Objective: 2

23. Knowing your weaknesses, and accepting them, is a characteristic of someone with a
    __________________ self-esteem.
    Answer: high   Difficulty: 1   Section: 1   Objective: 2

24 Someone who has a low self-esteem would be __________________ with their physical
    appearance.
    Answer: unhappy   Difficulty: 1   Section: 1   Objective: 3

25. As you grow as a person your self-esteem__________________, so you can build a more
    healthy self-esteem.
    Answer: changes   Difficulty: 2   Section: 1   Objective: 3

26. Your family can affect your self-esteem positively by providing__________________ for
    various activities you participate in.
    Answer: support   Difficulty: 1   Section: 1   Objective: 3

27. Encouragement helps build a _____________________ level of self-esteem.
    Answer: high   Difficulty: 1   Section: 1   Objective: 2

28. Peers can negatively impact your self-esteem by _____________________ you at school.
    Answer: teasing or bullying
            Difficulty: 1   Section: 1   Objective: 2

29. The way you see and imagine your body is called _____________________.
    Answer: body image   Difficulty: 1   Section: 1   Objective: 3

30. The way you see yourself as a person is called your _____________________.
    Answer: self-concept   Difficulty: 1   Section: 2   Objective: 1

31. Your self-concept can affect your self-esteem. A _____________________ self-concept will help you will keep a healthy level of self-esteem.
    Answer: positive   Difficulty: 1   Section: 2   Objective: 1

32. As you grow emotionally, your overall _____________________ will change.
    Answer: self-concept   Difficulty: 1   Section: 2   Objective: 1

33. Your ability to take responsibility for your actions is _____________________.
    Answer: integrity   Difficulty: 1   Section: 3   Objective: 1

34. Knowing what is _____________________ for you and what is_____________________ for you is called respecting yourself.
    Answer: right/wrong
            Difficulty: 1   Section: 3   Objective: 1

35. When you act on your thoughts and values in an honest and respectful way you are being _____________________.
    Answer: assertive   Difficulty: 1   Section: 3   Objective: 1

36. Media, by typically portraying only very successful and unusually attractive people, can negatively impact our own _____________________.
    Answer: body image   Difficulty: 1   Section: 1   Objective: 3

37. The measure of how much you value, respect, and feel confident about yourself is _____________________.
    Answer: self-esteem   Difficulty: 1   Section: 2   Objective: 1

38. The area of your personality called _____________________ is being use when you see yourself in comparison to your classmates.
    Answer: academic self-concept
            Difficulty: 1   Section: 2   Objective: 2

39. Your _____________________is how you see your physical abilities.
    Answer: physical self-concept
            Difficulty: 1   Section: 2   Objective: 2

40. How you see yourself in relationships is called your _____________________.
    Answer: social self-concept
            Difficulty: 1   Section: 2   Objective: 2

41. By knowing yourself you can build a healthy self-esteem. Knowing yourself means understanding what your _____________________ and your _____________________ are.
    Answer: strengths/weaknesses
            Difficulty: 1   Section: 3   Objective: 2

42. One of the seven ways to a healthy self-esteem is called "do something for others." The most important part of this step is your willingness to _____________________ your time, effort, and energy.
    Answer: volunteer   Difficulty: 1   Section: 3   Objective: 2

SHORT ANSWER

43. What is body image?

    Answer: Body image is how you see and imagine your body.

    Difficulty: 1   Section: 1   Objective: 3

44. Define self-esteem.

    Sample answer:
    Self-esteem is how much you like yourself as a person. It is how you feel and respect yourself.

    Difficulty: 2   Section: 1   Objective: 1

45. How might comparing yourself to an image in the media lead to an unhealthy self-esteem?

    Sample answer:
    People who compare themselves to the people they see in the media may develop unhealthy body images if they are nor comfortable with their own bodies.

    Difficulty: 2   Section: 1   Objective: 2, 3

46. What are some characteristics of a person with a high self-esteem?

    Sample answer:
    They feel good about themselves, know their strengths and weaknesses, accept who they are, and they like themselves.

    Difficulty: 2   Section: 1   Objective: 2

47. As your self-esteem develops it is influenced by many factors. List three factors that would impact your self-esteem.

    Sample answer: family, friends, teachers, and or coaches

    Difficulty: 2   Section: 1   Objective: 3

48. Self concept is a part of self-esteem. Explain how self-concept is different from self-esteem.

    Answer:
    Self-concept is the way you imagine and see yourself as a person. Self-esteem is how you feel about yourself. Self-concept is a part of your self-esteem.

    Difficulty: 2   Section: 2   Objective: 1

49. What does it mean to build good character?

    Answer:
    There are three key ways to build good character and a healthy self-esteem. They are, integrity, respecting yourself, and being assertive.

    Difficulty: 2   Section: 3   Objective: 1

50. Knowing your strengths or positive qualities refers to which of the seven ways to build a higher level of self-esteem?

    Answer: get to know yourself

    Difficulty: 2   Section: 3   Objective: 2

51. Accepting your appearance and not wanting to change your personality refers to which of the seven ways to build self-esteem?

    Answer: accept yourself

    Difficulty: 1   Section: 3   Objective: 2

52. Explain how the media can impact your level of self-esteem?

    Sample answer:
    Displaying body images which are not typical can lead to frustration resulting in a lower self-esteem because of an inabiity to achieve such an ideal body image.

    Difficulty: 2   Section: 1   Objective: 3

53. List seven ways to improve your self-esteem?
    Answer:
    get to know yourself, accept yourself, be good at something, set a goal, be positive, turn problems into challenges, do something for others
    Difficulty: 2   Section: 3   Objective: 2

54. Which one of the seven ways to healthy self-esteem means being comfortable with your appearance?
    Answer: accept yourself
    Difficulty: 1   Section: 3   Objective: 2

55. Which one of the seven ways to healthy self-esteem means acquiring a sense of accomplishment by following a plan to fruition?
    Answer: set a goal   Difficulty: 1   Section: 3   Objective: 2

56. Which one of the seven ways to healthy self-esteem means being your own personal cheerleader?
    Answer: be positive   Difficulty: 1   Section: 3   Objective: 2

57. What is integrity?
    Answer: Integrityis being honest and taking responsibilty
    Difficulty: 1   Section: 3   Objective: 1

58. Give three examples of things that you would refuse in order to show self-respect.
    Sample answer:
    refusing drugs, alcohol, tobacco, refusing to cheat or skip class
    Difficulty: 2   Section: 3   Objective: 2

59. How is being assertive different from being aggressive?
    Sample answer:
    Being assertive means acting on your values without making people feel bad. Being aggressive leaves other people feeliing bad.
    Difficulty: 2   Section: 3   Objective: 1

60. Does accepting yourself mean that you don't want to change your personality at all?
    Sample answer:
    No, accepting yourself means that you like certain parts of your personality, but that you are willing to accept or even change some of the things you don't like about your pesonality.
    Difficulty: 2   Section: 3   Objective: 2

MATCHING

a. encouragement	d. media
b. family	e. peers
c. body image	f. self-doubt

61. ____ the way you see and imagine your body
    Answer: C   Difficulty: 1   Section: 1   Objective: 3
62. ____ includes TV, magazines, movies, and music videos
    Answer: D   Difficulty: 1   Section: 1   Objective: 3
63. ____ people who are generally in your own age group
    Answer: E   Difficulty: 1   Section: 1   Objective: 3
64. ____ can help build self-esteem
    Answer: A   Difficulty: 1   Section: 1   Objective: 3
65. ____ factor which influences self-esteem
    Answer: B   Difficulty: 1   Section: 1   Objective: 3

a. get to know yourself
b. accept yourself
c. be good at something
d. set a goal

e. be positive
f. turn problems into challenges
g. do something for others

66. ____ volunteering

Answer: G   Difficulty: 1   Section: 3   Objective: 2

67. ____ dealing with disappointment in a positive way

Answer: F   Difficulty: 1   Section: 3   Objective: 2

68. ____ being your own personal cheerleader

Answer: E   Difficulty: 1   Section: 3   Objective: 2

69. ____ knowing your strengths

Answer: A   Difficulty: 1   Section: 3   Objective: 2

70. ____ not wanting change your personality too much.

Answer: B   Difficulty: 1   Section: 3   Objective: 2

71. ____ choose an acivity you would like to do well

Answer: C   Difficulty: 1   Section: 3   Objective: 2

72. ____ find your strengths

Answer: D   Difficulty: 1   Section: 3   Objective: 2

a. self-concept
b. physical self-concept

c. academic self concept
d. social self-concept

73. ____ seeing yourself as a good friend

Answer: D   Difficulty: 1   Section: 2   Objective: 2

74. ____ seeing yourself as a student

Answer: C   Difficulty: 1   Section: 2   Objective: 2

75. seeing yourself as an average athlete

Answer: B   Difficulty: 1   Section: 2   Objective: 2

76. ____ can help build self-esteem

Answer: A   Difficulty: 1   Section: 2   Objective: 2

ESSAY

77. Marisa gets together every week with a group of friends who watch their favorite television show. The group of six girls are really into the characters. So much so that two of Marisa's friends are starting to worry her. Julie wants to be a s popular as her favorite character on the show and says she is ready to start taking risks to make herself more mature. She's finding it hard to accept who she is. And, Lisa, who is a really smart and nice person, feels she is too heavy. Marisa thinks she's just right, but Lisa believes differntly and is considering taking diet pills like her favorirte character on the show. Marisa thinks she's okay, but she' been after her brother to wear designer clothes and get a more fashionable haircut, just like her favorite male character from the show. What should Marisa tell her friends? What should they tell her?

Sample answer:
    Answers should include the concept that media tends to show only people who are very successful and unusually attractive.

Difficulty: 2   Section: 1   Objective: 2

78. Asking questions and trying new things are ways to get to know yourself better. What questions should you ask yourself to get a better handle on who you are and to answer the question, "Do you have healthy self-esteem?"

Sample answer:
    What kinds of things do I like to do? What kinds of things don't I like, what are my strengths, or positive qualities, what are my weaknesses

Difficulty: 2   Section: 3   Objective: 2

79. The numbers of students suffering from anorexia nervosa and bulimia nervosa in an attempt to control their body iamge has increased significantly over the past couple of years. In media advertisements, TV shows, and music videos characters are very thin, with very athletic bodies, wear the latest fashions, and drive the coolest cars. What would you say to a friend who said to you, "I would do anything to be like them."?

Sample answer:
> You would tell them that the media tends to show only people who are very successful and unusually attractive. Often times we fail to know the person behind the image who may have a low self-esteem off camera. A healthy self-esteem comes from having integrity, respecting yourself, and being assertive, not trying to be someone else.

Difficulty: 2   Section: 1   Objective: 3

80. Why does doing something for others build healthy self-esteem? What would you say to a friend who thought it was strange for you to suggest that you both volunteer your time to help homeless people?

Sample answer:
> Very few things make you feel as good as helping those who may be less fortunate. The increased confidence you will get from the little time you give will be well worth the boost to your self-esteem.

Difficulty: 2   Section: 3   Objective: 2

CONCEPT MAP

81. Use the following terms to create a concept map: *family, grow emotionally, friends, self-esteem, teachers, coaches,* and *influenced*

Answer:
> *Self esteem* changes as you *grow emotionally* and can be *influenced* by *family, friends, teachers, coaches.*

Difficulty: 2   Section: 1   Objective: 2